Dear High School Senior, Prepare for Life After School

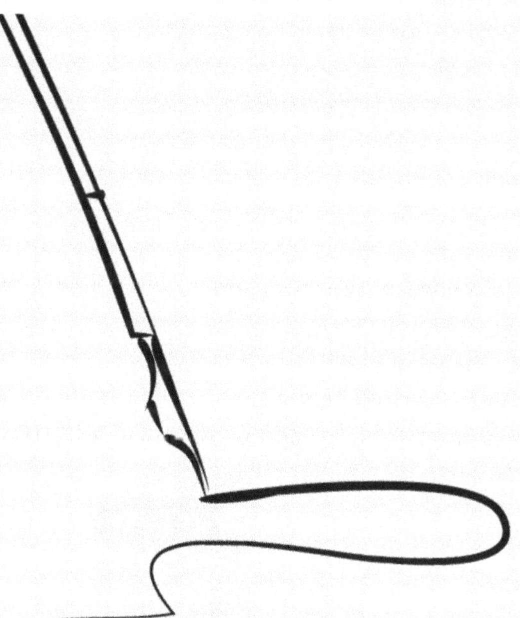

Nicole Herbert Dean

Thinkologie

What is Thinkologie?

Thinkologie is an educational content brand, conceived by Nicole Herbert Dean.

Nicole has been an educational consultant and coach since the late nineties. She specializes in foreign and English as a Second language, culture, and life skills.

She has written curricula for the Defense Language Institute, Baltimore County Public Schools, the University of Maryland, and other government and private entities.

Having taught mostly virtually, Nicole has also coached educators, budding authors, and linguists on how to transition to the digital world.

Thinkologie includes coaching materials, curricula, story workbooks, vocabulary coloring books, college planners, worksheets, and digital activities.

Thinkologie educational resources are available on Amazon, Teachers Pay Teachers, Book Learning, and Gumroad.

Check the last page for contact information. We take custom orders for resources.

Create a Culturally Competent Life

Thinkologie

Dear High School Senior,

Whether you are going to college, trade school, or just a job, this little guide has my two-penny advice and some templates for you to organize your life after school.

Surprise everyone and start adulting early!

It is my hope that this book will help prepare you for life after high school.

I would love some feedback too! Help this coach out!

Ms. Nicole Herbert Dean

Going out on your own!

This time cannot come soon enough for some of you!

Some of you may be going to college, moving in with your significant other, or sharing a home with a few friends.

Still, others may continue to live with your parents. Hey! Nothing wrong with that! I am sure you are saving those dollars to get your own place.

Well, this is the most exciting time in your life. But it is also the most crucial!

The habits you develop living independently can make you wealthy in the long run, or make you broke.

You want to hit the ground running with your plan to be independent.

This book can help guide you in that direction.

We have prompted planners templates for everything, from setting up your home, roommate agreements, debt and savings trackers, etc.

Print out the planners and place them in a binder to use them.

Moving out?
Scary but exciting!

As with any real estate decision - renting or buying, and moving out on your own is scary but exciting.

If you are not living on campus, make sure you choose your abode with care.

Seek a safe neighborhood.

Check out the neighborhood during the day as well as the night before you move in.

Find and choose your roommates with caution. Even close friendships can go sour when you live together.

Make a checklist of what you will need beforehand.

Check out the parking or transportation situation. Those tickets or payments can add up.

Talk with people who have lived in that place before. Real stories are better than reviews. But check the reviews too.

Make sure everything is working inside and outside the home.

New Home To Do's

PEOPLE TO CALL

- [ ]
- [ ]

THINGS TO CLEAN

- [ ]
- [ ]
- [ ]
- [ ]
- [ ]
- [ ]

THINGS TO REMOVE

- [ ]
- [ ]
- [ ]
- [ ]
- [ ]
- [ ]

THINGS TO SELL

- [ ]
- [ ]
- [ ]
- [ ]
- [ ]
- [ ]

THINGS TO BUY

- [ ]
- [ ]
- [ ]
- [ ]
- [ ]
- [ ]

THINGS TO FIX

- [ ]
- [ ]
- [ ]
- [ ]
- [ ]
- [ ]

NEW THINGS TO PLAN

- [ ]
- [ ]
- [ ]
- [ ]
- [ ]
- [ ]

Choose your roommate carefully!

A great roommate can make your adulting experience fantastic as you create new memories with them.

But, a nightmare roommate can make what would otherwise be one of the best times in your timeline, a disaster!

So, choose your roommate with caution. Trust is an important factor. After all, this person is going to be privy to your privacy.

Things to look for in a roommate:

- Are they clean?
- Are they responsible when it comes to paying the rent, or will they skimp on bills?
- Are they trustworthy?
- Do their sleep habits gel with yours?

Once you have chosen whom to live with, define things in writing.

Create a roommate agreement.

Check out our template for this on the next page.

Then set the chores list for each one.

Print it out and stick it on the fridge.

Set a date for the last week of the month for the rent due.

Delegate one person to hand over the rent to the landlord.

Have a little jar for roommate shenanigans!

Bonding time or getaway-from-schoolwork times are important!

Roommate Agreement

Get Things Done Now, Not Later

Don't put off stuff. Tackle them as soon as you possibly can. And get things done.

Procrastination never helped anyone. You will forget stuff if you put it off for later.

Seize opportunities.

They say that the busier you are the more you get things done.

Make a to-do list. Arrange them in order of priority and due date. Then tackle the list.

A good practice is to review assignments due, meetings, errands to run, oil changes, etc that are on your calendar every Monday morning.

Set reminders on your phone. If you tend to ignore the reminders, set alarms to remind you.

Use the template on the next page as a guide.

Get Things Done

TOP PRIORITIES FOR THE DAY

CHORES

cleaning up

wash the dishes

make the bed

feed the pets

laundry

WATER

TO-DO

THINGS TO DO TOMORROW

FOOD

BREAKFAST

LUNCH

DINNER

APPOINTMENTS

PHONE /EMAIL

FITNESS

NOTES

MOOD SKETCH

Chores List

	Chores	Frequency	Person in Charge
1			
2			
3			
4			
5			
6			
7			
8			
9			
10			
11			
12			

So Many Options......And there is so little time.

You have just graduated from high school.

You probably have had several summer jobs and after-school jobs by now.

Here is the thing, you don't have to have it all figured out.

One thing at a time.

I recommend taking an aptitude test if you have not done so.

Understanding who you are and how you function is the first step.

A few options:

Myers Briggs Personality Test

Maslow

Heck, even one course at a time is good. But get a skill.

Get several!

Go to a trade school if you don't want to go to a four-year college.

Pick up an apprenticeship and earn money while you learn.

Study what you love to do.

And do it!

However, a key point to remember is that no job is perfect. No job is all fun all the time.

There are parts to every job that may be mundane or boring. But all the same, do what you enjoy doing as this is where you will spend most of your waking life.

Have a Career Plan

Plan Period

Current job

Goals

Short Term | Mid Term | Long Term

How I will make it happen

Current Skills | New Skills Wish List

Create a Good Resume

A resume is a document that you prepare to present your education, skills, background and experience to employers.

Create a resume and update it every year.

Make sure to update and add each stage of your education, each new job or a new skill.

We have created a handy editable resume template for you. Edit and use the resume template on the next page as a guide.

Add a cover letter to it and you are good to go!

Save Documents

My dad collected all my report cards, birth certificate, awards, and any other document pertaining to me in a large binder. He would make copies of each and insert them with the originals in sheet protectors.

I still have it and have preserved all my important documents.

Nowadays, you can also save a digital copy of each document in the cloud. Google cloud or iCloud is a great place.

It is safe to have both a hard copy and a digital copy of your documents.

Digital copies stored in the cloud can provide access from anywhere.

This is an excellent practice as you will have them handy and all in one place through the years as you go through life.

YOUR NAME

W E B   D E V E L O P E R

123-456-7890

hello@reallygreatsite.com

123 Anywhere St., Any City

reallygreatsite.com

PROFILE

I am a qualified and professional web developer with five years of experience in database administration and website design. Strong creative and analytical skills. Team player with an eye for detail.

SKILLS

- Web Design
- Design Thinking
- Wireframe Creation
- Front End Coding
- Problem-Solving
- Computer Literacy
- Project Management Tools
- Strong Communication

EXPERIENCE

APPLICATIONS DEVELOPER
Really Great Company
2016 - Present

- Database administration and website design
- Built the logic for a streamlined ad-serving platform that scaled
- Educational institutions and online classroom management

WEB CONTENT MANAGER
Really Great Company
2014 - 2016

- Database administration and website design
- Built the logic for a streamlined ad-serving platform that scaled
- Educational institutions and online classroom management

ANALYSIS CONTENT
Really Great Company
2010 - 2014

- Database administration and website design
- Built the logic for a streamlined ad-serving platform that scaled
- Educational institutions and online classroom management

EDUCATION

SECONDARY SCHOOL
Really Great High School
2010 - 2014

BACHELOR OF TECHNOLOGY
Really Great University
2014 - 2016

Plan Ahead for Finals Week

If you are in college or trade school, make sure you do the following before and during your finals, or any test or interview:

- get a good night's sleep, every night
- drink lots of water, it keeps you alert
- eat properly at set times
- make sure you get enough proteins and fiber
- remove distractions - include the significant other in this one!
- turn off the tv if you can
- set times for phone time - if you cannot go off grid

Finals Planning Tracker

TO-DO

- [ ]
- [ ]
- [ ]
- [ ]
- [ ]
- [ ]
- [ ]
- [ ]
- [ ]
- [ ]
- [ ]
- [ ]
- [ ]
- [ ]

NOTES

MONDAY

TUESDAY

WEDNESDAY

THURSDAY

FRIDAY

SATURDAY/SUNDAY

Finals Planning Tracker

TO-DO

- [ ]
- [ ]
- [ ]
- [ ]
- [ ]
- [ ]
- [ ]
- [ ]
- [ ]
- [ ]
- [ ]
- [ ]
- [ ]
- [ ]

NOTES

MONDAY

TUESDAY

WEDNESDAY

THURSDAY

FRIDAY

SATURDAY/SUNDAY

Read, Read, Read!

there are many benefits to reading every day. Besides providing knowledge, reading stimulates your brain and retains its power as you grow older.

Reading enhances learning, stimulates the brain, helps in problem-solving (think mystery novels), and helps in critical and analytical thinking.

Reading also slows the onset of Alzheimer's and Dementia and improves focus and concentration.

Reading brings in calm to this fast-paced world with its endless scrolling and stimulation.

Did you know that the average millionaire who is self-made reads 2 books at least a month?

Elon Musk attributes a lot of his success to reading books.

Reading opens up your world to endless possibilities.

If a book is too boring, get magazines such as the New Yorker, New York Times Magazine, Architectural Digest, and other publications.

I am a writer but I can honestly say I read more than I write.

A lot of my inspiration comes from reading.

Create and curate lists of genres you like to read and have monthly goals to finish the books.

Reading List

TITLE	AUTHOR	GENRE	DATE	RATING
				☆☆☆☆☆
				☆☆☆☆☆
				☆☆☆☆☆
				☆☆☆☆☆
				☆☆☆☆☆
				☆☆☆☆☆
				☆☆☆☆☆
				☆☆☆☆☆
				☆☆☆☆☆
				☆☆☆☆☆
				☆☆☆☆☆
				☆☆☆☆☆
				☆☆☆☆☆
				☆☆☆☆☆
				☆☆☆☆☆
				☆☆☆☆☆
				☆☆☆☆☆
				☆☆☆☆☆
				☆☆☆☆☆
				☆☆☆☆☆
				☆☆☆☆☆
				☆☆☆☆☆
				☆☆☆☆☆
				☆☆☆☆☆

Reading List

TITLE	AUTHOR	GENRE	DATE	RATING

Finances

It is not how much money you make, but how much you get to keep at the end of the day.

Saving should become a habit.

Between the college loan, rent and car expenses, you want to have money to play with, right?

Check out our template for prioritizing your moolah spending!

Use the Bill trackers, Savings and Debt tracker to monitor your cash.

Keep track of all the apps you are subscribed to! They can be sneaky, eating away at your cash flow.

List out what you would like to purchase in order of priority, needs or wants. The priorities are things you have to have - e.g. a good working car, gas, a roof over your head, food etc. Then list out the needs - you need a good pair of shoes and decent clothes. The wants would be that video game or new make up?

Priorities	Needs	Wants

Bills Tracker

Bills		Month											
Bill	Unit	1	2	3	4	5	6	7	8	9	10	11	12

Savings - Start it immediately!

My mother always said, "It's not about the money you make, but it is about the money you get to keep."

Start saving right from the very first time you receive money. If you have a dollar try to save at least half.

Put it away where you cannot access it easily.

You will be amazed at how much you will have collected at the end of the year.

Tips for saving:

Treat yourself to your favorite barista coffee just once a week instead of every day.

Have your friends over and cook together instead of ordering pizza. It is a fun activity and you save a ton of money.

Eat out with friends only once or twice a month. Saves on gas as well as restaurant bills.

Every time you get more than five one-dollar bills, save the excess dollars in a jar. This is a fun game!

Cancel any app subscriptions you are not using.

Wait at least two weeks on the impulse to buy - anything.

Unplug those phone chargers, gaming equipment, etc when you are not using them.

Savings Tracker

Date	Deposit	Amount

Date	Deposit	Amount

Debt Tracker

Account:

Credit Limit: Interest Due:

Minimum Due: Due Date:

BALANCE	PAYMENT	DATE	NEW BALANCE

Subscription Tracker

Organisation	Date Paid	Amount	Duration	Exp.Date	Method of renewal	Renewal Date

Plan your meals

Planning saves time and works well with your wallet. If you have no time to go into a detailed plan then at least figure out the main food item you will want to eat each day.

A great option is also to plan and share meals with a roommate. This will motivate you to cook. Plus you will always remember trying out that dish that you loved. Have a nicely set table. Be present in the moment and savor the food. Homework or paperwork can wait.

Have your pantry stocked with items that you know you will need every week. Things like pasta or rice, lentils, beans, and soups keep for a while.

Breakfast essentials like milk, eggs, and butter are also great to buy and refrigerate. Eating at least one healthy meal especially breakfast can set the tone for your day. You won't be hungry at work or class.

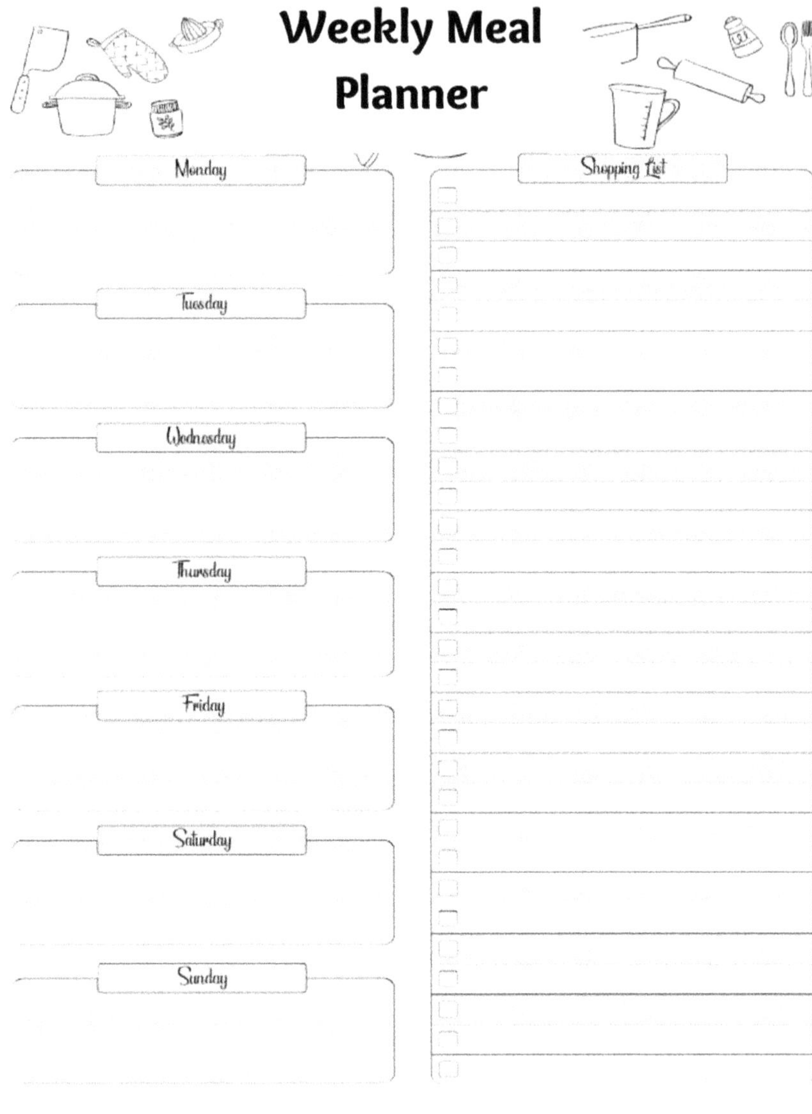

Weekly Meal Planner
Monday
Tuesday
Wednesday
Thursday
Friday
Saturday
Sunday
Shopping List

Weekly Meal Planner

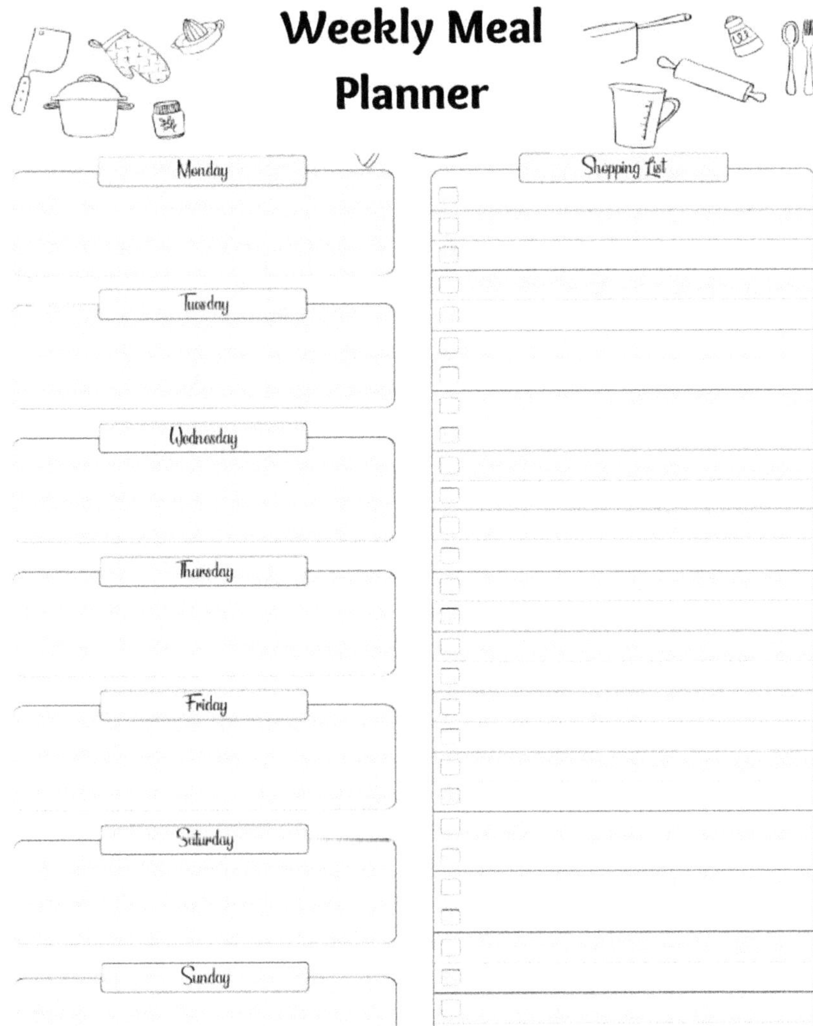

Weekly Meal Planner

Monday

Tuesday

Wednesday

Thursday

Friday

Saturday

Sunday

Shopping List

Weekly Meal Planner

Monday

Tuesday

Wednesday

Thursday

Friday

Saturday

Sunday

Shopping List

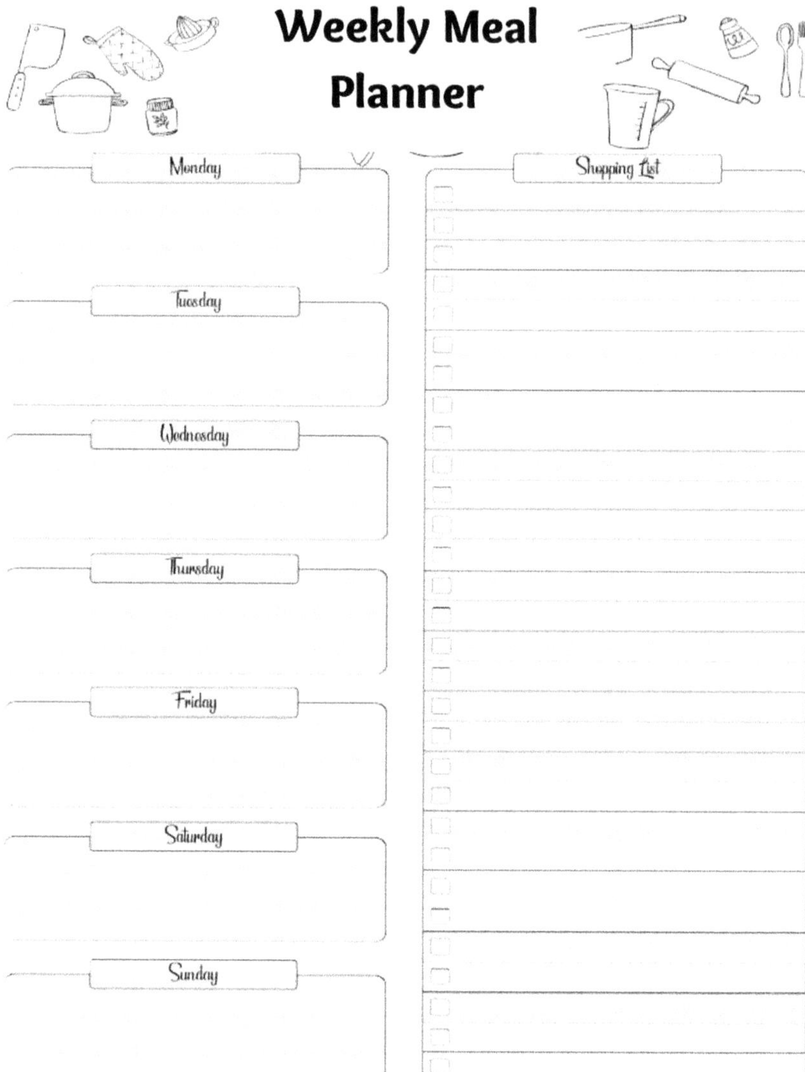

Weekly Meal Planner

Monday

Tuesday

Wednesday

Thursday

Friday

Saturday

Sunday

Shopping List

Recipe

Ingredients

Notes

Recipe

Ingredients

Notes

Recipe

Ingredients

Notes

Recipe

Ingredients

Notes

Recipe

Ingredients

Notes

Don't Forget Your Family or Friends

Leaving family can be hard but besides the text messages, Face Times and phone calls - send cards by snail mail.

Classy and thoughtful! It will impress them that you took the time to write it out and go to the post office and mail it.

Use the Birthday Reminder lists to remind you of important birthdays in your family or friends.

Buy a box of assorted cards at the beginning of the year to send by old fashioned snail mail.

Birthday Reminder

January	February	March
April	May	June
July	August	September
October	November	December

Birthday Reminder

January	February	March
April	May	June
July	August	September
October	November	December

Mental Health and Self Care

Moving out can be an exciting experience but it can get interesting if you do not have family or friends close by. Having a good support system is necessary no matter where you are in the world.

Make sure you develop some good close friendships with people who are reliable and trustworthy.

Knowing you are not alone, is key. Have someone you can talk with about anything and everything.

This cannot be stressed enough. Studies show that our physical health is directly related to our state of mind.

Put yourself first. You can be replaced at your job. You can replace and make up money. But you cannot replace time. Time lost in carelessness when it comes to health is detrimental.

Take time out everyday to do little mental health activities. Have a strategy to carve out even 5 minutes of your schedule.

You won't regret it.

Self-care Plan

Goals for my mind

- ....
- ....
- ....
- ....

Mind

Mental health
Mindfulness and self knowledge

Soul
Stimulation and fulfillment

Goals for my body

- ....
- ....
- ....
- ....

Body

Self-care
Basic hygiene and body care

Improvement
Exercise, sleep and healthy food

Good rules & habits i want to live by

Soul Stuff Notes

Instruction

Fill these space with your favorite activities & things to fall back on when you're in a bad mood and having a not-so-good day.

My favorite

Favorite Movies

....

....

....

Favorite Books

....

....

....

Favorite Games

....

....

....

Things I do when I'm sad

....

....

....

Things i do when i'm Bored

....

....

....

This year i'm looking forward to

30 Self-care Challenges

○ Stretch all your muscles	○ Drink more water	○ Go for a walk in nature	○ Indulge in your favorite treat	○ Go to bed earlier
○ Listen to favorite song	○ Eat vegetarian meals	○ Take a nice bubble bath	○ Cook your favorite meal	○ Practice yoga
○ Go on a solo date	○ Journaling	○ Give yourself a facial	○ Practice gratitude	○ Try a DIY Project
○ Watch the sunrise	○ Read a book	○ Explore a new city	○ Watch your favorite movie	○ Give yourself a manicure
○ Get some sunlight	○ Start a new hobby	○ Write out your goals	○ Organize your closet	○ Watch the sunset
○ Give yourself a break	○ Learn a new skill	○ Create your ideal future	○ Surround yourself with positivity	○ Drink plenty of water

30 Self-care Challenges

○ Stretch all your muscles	○ Drink more water	○ Go for a walk in nature	○ Indulge in your favorite treat	○ Go to bed earlier
○ Listen to favorite song	○ Eat vegetarian meals	○ Take a nice bubble bath	○ Cook your favorite meal	○ Practice yoga
○ Go on a solo date	○ Journaling	○ Give yourself a facial	○ Practice gratitude	○ Try a DIY Project
○ Watch the sunrise	○ Read a book	○ Explore a new city	○ Watch your favorite movie	○ Give yourself a manicure
○ Get some sunlight	○ Start a new hobby	○ Write out your goals	○ Organize your closet	○ Watch the sunset
○ Give yourself a break	○ Learn a new skill	○ Create your ideal future	○ Surround yourself with positivity	○ Drink plenty of water

My Dear Future Self

Today's Date

....

Instruction

Writing a letter to your future self is a fun exercise that lets you reflect on your current life, as well as your goals and dreams.

Decide how old do you want your future self to be when you read this letter and store it somewhere save until then.

Dear me,

Sincerely,
Myself

Contact us

Our mission is to help other educators, coaches and homeschoolers also!

Contact us for customized interactive books. If you want to publish your book - contact us for that too!

Follow our author page

https://amazon.com/author/thinkologiebooks

We are also on Instagram @thinkologie

Twitter @ thinkologie

Facebook @thinkologiemedia

www.ingramcontent.com/pod-product-compliance
Ingram Content Group UK Ltd.
Pitfield, Milton Keynes, MK11 3LW, UK
UKHW022009190726
13853UKWH00004B/1831